I am praying

find *comfort* in knowing

*who you belong to* and that

there is no greater calling

or claim on your life.

Let your heart *rest* in

God's presence—what He is

doing is best!

Peace is the calm assurance
that what God is doing is best.

*James MacDonald*

You are *victorious!*

I am praying you remember

who is *fighting for you* and

with you, and who goes after

you. The God of *peace* will

*sustain* you, and His grace is

sufficient in your weakness.

The God of peace will soon crush
Satan under your feet. The grace
of our Lord Jesus be with you.

ROMANS 16:20 NIV

To me, it has been a source of great comfort
and strength in the day of battle, just to
remember that the secret of steadfastness,
and indeed, of victory, is the recognition
that "the Lord is at hand."

*Duncan Campbell*

I am praying that you *take refuge* in the confident hope you have been called to. Don't let this world keep you in a box or make you feel small. You have a rich and *glorious inheritance!*

I pray that your hearts will be flooded with light so that you can understand the confident hope He has given to those He called—His holy people who are His rich and glorious inheritance.

EPHESIANS 1:18 NLT

There is no sin too great for God's grace.
There is no habit too big for His healing.
There is no label too strong for His love.

*Craig Groeschel*

I am praying that no matter what life throws your way, you remember that *God is at work* in it all. In both the *blessings* and the burdens, He is your *help* and your *Provider*.

Truly my soul finds rest in God;
my salvation comes from Him.

PSALM 62:1 NIV

When we discover the secret of
being inwardly at worship while
outwardly at work, we find that the
soul's silence brings us to God and
God to us. Silence takes us beyond the
limits of consciousness and into the
heart and mind and will of God.

*Brent Bill*

Right on time, that is
God. I am praying that
you experience His *power*
and *kindness*, even when
circumstances are not what
you expect. He is watching.
*Take heart!*

Don't presume to know what God
is doing in your pain. Just know
that if you are His, He is only
ever doing you good.

*Kathryn Butler*

Today, I am praying that you are *comforted* by the knowledge of your *eternal home*. Don't be weary or fear the brokenness around you; we are all just passing through, but our *hearts are seated* in heavenly realms.

We know that if the tent that is our earthly home is destroyed, we have a building from God, a house not made with hands, eternal in the heavens.

II CORINTHIANS 5:1 ESV

I have held many things in my hands, and have lost them all; but whatever I have placed in God's hands, that I still possess.

*Martin Luther*

DaySpring

*Peace*—the greatest
gift. I am praying your
mind is recalibrated with
the *truth* and *joy* of Jesus.
His way for your life is *peace*.

> You will keep in perfect peace
> those whose minds are steadfast,
> because they trust in You.
>
> ISAIAH 26:3 NIV

If you don't have peace, it isn't
because someone took it from you;
you gave it away. You cannot always
control what happens to you, but you
can control what happens in you.

*John Maxwell*

I am praying you'll find a *safe space* with *Jesus*, your *Savior* and your *strength*. The storm will never overtake the Creator of the seas.

He replied, "You of little faith, why are you so afraid?" Then He got up and rebuked the winds and the waves, and it was completely calm. The men were amazed and asked, "What kind of man is this? Even the winds and the waves obey Him!"

MATTHEW 8:26–27 NIV

What we choose to use as our anchor determines how well we will weather the seasons of life.

*Lauren Chandler*

The *Giver of hope*
is always with you.

I am praying that God's
*joy, peace, and hope*
overflow into all parts
of your life.

May the God of hope fill you with all
joy and peace as you trust in Him,
so that you may overflow with hope
by the power of the Holy Spirit.

ROMANS 15:13 NIV

We've been designed as a resting
place for the spirit of God,
changing every environment we
walk into.

*Bill Johnson*

I am praying that you are able to *slow down* and walk *step by step* with Jesus. Let the pressure be on His shoulders and your *faith* will soar.

Consider the lilies, how they grow: they neither toil nor spin, yet I tell you, even Solomon in all his glory was not arrayed like one of these. But if God so clothes the grass, which is alive in the field today, and tomorrow is thrown into the oven, how much more will he clothe you, O you of little faith!

LUKE 12:27–28 ESV

You must not give way to fears and doubts, but let faith answer them with Scripture.

*Matthew Henry*

*Renewed,* that is

God's promise to you.

I am praying you always take

any discouragement to the

*Source of all hope* and your

*strength* will be restored.

> Those who hope in the LORD will renew
> their strength. They will soar on wings
> like eagles; they will run and not grow
> weary, they will walk and not be faint.
>
> ISAIAH 40:31 NIV

Rest time is not waste time.
It is economy to gather fresh
strength.... It is wisdom to
take occasional furlough.
In the long run, we shall do
more by sometimes doing less.

*Charles Spurgeon*

Isn't it incredible

and hard to believe that

the *King of kings* has

made His home in *your heart?*

Praying you are *encouraged*

by this *truth* in every

moment you face.

We can be tired, weary,
and emotionally distraught,
but after spending time alone with
God, we find that He injects into our
bodies energy, power, and strength.

*Charles Stanley*

DaySpring

I am praying that the anthem of *"God's got this"* repeats throughout your mind and your heart today. When His *peace* rules our hearts, we rule our days with *gratitude and grace.*

Let the peace of Christ rule in your hearts, since as members of one body you were called to peace. And be thankful.

COLOSSIANS 3:15 NIV

Seek God's guidance. Leave the outcomes to Him. Enjoy the peace of understanding that "God's got this."

*Faye Horton*

DaySpring

*Thankful* for the way you bring *peace* to every situation you encounter. God finds so much *delight* in watching His children operate in *peace* that is beyond all understanding, knowing they are *trusting* in Him.

Peacemakers who sow in peace reap a harvest of righteousness.

JAMES 3:18 NIV

When our souls are healthy we change the environment, the environment doesn't change us.

*Carl Lentz*

If God is your priority,

then it does not matter if

the world is in chaos around

you. You can walk in *peace*.

I am praying that your heart

is *comforted* and *eased* today

as you remember God is in

*control* of all things.

> God is not a God of disorder but
> of peace, as in all the meetings
> of God's holy people.
>
> I CORINTHIANS 14:33 NLT

We must settle in our hearts that
no matter what, God is sovereign.

*Beth Moore*

Jesus is in your boat and *peace* is yours! Praying you feel His *presence close* today, knowing that no matter the winds and the waves that crash around, He is the *calm within you.*

Then He arose and rebuked the wind, and said to the sea, "Peace, be still!" And the wind ceased and there was a great calm.

MARK 4:39 NKJV

Peace doesn't come from finding a lake with no storms. It comes from having Jesus in the boat.

*John Ortberg*

I am praying you
are able to rest in
the *peace* God provides
and the *joy* that accompanies
having a *peaceful heart.*

For the things we see now will
soon be gone, but the things we
cannot see will last forever.

II CORINTHIANS 4:18 NLT

Anything that undermines your
peace ultimately undermines
your happiness.

*Andy Stanley*

DaySpring

I'm praying God continues to reveal more and more of His *amazing* ways to you. Your plans will be known in time!

> I count everything as loss because of the surpassing worth of knowing Christ Jesus my Lord. For his sake I have suffered the loss of all things and count them as rubbish, in order that I may gain Christ.
>
> PHILIPPIANS 3:8 ESV

The Father doesn't give life directions in one big bundle because the goal is knowing Him, not the plan.

*Louie Giglio*

I am praying God

will shed light on His

*fingerprints in your life*

and the lives of others today!

When you focus on you and

what you lack, life will

always feel heavy.

Praying you clearly see all

the ways He is *lifting you up.*

For what does it profit a man if he gains the
whole world and loses or forfeits himself?

LUKE 9:25 ESV

You're exhausted in the faith because
you're looking at you. The more you look
at yourself and the less you look at God,
the more you get frustrated at yourself.

*Matt Chandler*

Wherever you are, *God is there.* I am praying you'll hear Him speak clearly today.

He has things to tell you today—to *uplift* you, *strengthen* you, and give you *peace.*

Continue steadfastly in prayer, being watchful in it with thanksgiving.

COLOSSIANS 4:2 ESV

There is a vast difference between talking about God and listening to a God who talks to you.

*Lisa Bevere*

Isn't it so *comforting* to know that no matter what goes on around us, *calmness* can remain inside of us? Praying His *peace* permeates your soul today.

> There is no fear in love,
> but perfect love casts out fear.
>
> I JOHN 4:18 ESV

Calmness sets in making me
aware of God's love so abundantly.

*Judy Harrell*

*Beautiful*, that is you,

on the inside and out.

As you are still with God,

I am praying you will begin

to see yourself as He sees

you. His *love* is *pursuing*

your heart.

> "Though the mountains be shaken and
> the hills be removed, yet My unfailing
> love for you will not be shaken nor My
> covenant of peace be removed," says the
> LORD, who has compassion on you.
>
> ISAIAH 54:10 NIV

God's love looks for those who
feel unlovely, desiring to make
them beautiful again.

*Natalie Grant*

Big or small, I am *praying* that you bring it to the feet of Jesus. May you *be still and know* that King Jesus is at work in your life.

Come, let us worship and bow down.
Let us kneel before the LORD our Maker.

PSALM 95:6 NLT

Every great movement of God can be traced to a kneeling figure.

*Dwight L. Moody*

I am praying you'll
*find peace* in knowing
you don't have to figure
it all out; you can trust
God to bring all things to
*completion* and *rest easy*
in His arms.

I am sure of this, that he
who began a good work in you
will bring it to completion at
the day of Jesus Christ.

PHILIPPIANS 1:6 ESV

God is more interested in your future
and your relationships than you are.

*Billy Graham*

God is taking all your sufferings and giving you an *unwavering joy* and *perseverance*.
I am praying you'll feel His presence overcome you today.

But to the degree that you share the sufferings of Christ, keep on rejoicing, so that also at the revelation of His glory you may rejoice with exultation.

I PETER 4:13 NASB

Let God's promises shine on your problems.

*Corrie ten Boom*

God has never and will

never leave your side.

I am praying you will feel

the *assurance* of His *care,*

the *beauty* of His *perspective,*

and the *power* of His *hope* in

your life today.

This I call to mind, and therefore
I have hope: The steadfast love of the
Lord never ceases; his mercies never
come to an end; they are new every
morning; great is your faithfulness.

LAMENTATIONS 3:21-23 ESV

Joy doesn't come when you try to hold
it all together. Joy comes when you
let God hold you.

*Unknown*

I am asking God to *give you great comfort* as you take *refuge* in Him.

This God—his way is perfect; the word
of the LORD proves true; he is a shield
for all those who take refuge in him.

II SAMUEL 22:31 ESV

Have you been asking God what
He is going to do? He will never
tell you. God does not tell you
what He is going to do; He reveals
to you Who He is.

*Oswald Chambers*

DaySpring

I am praying you find time to just sit and be with Jesus today. Soak up how much you are *loved* and how *important* you are to Him. That changes everything.

Time spent alone with God is not wasted. It changes us; it changes our surroundings; and every Christian who would live the life that counts, and who would have power for service, must take time to pray.

*M. E. Andross*

When we are quiet and still before Jesus, our shame disappears. He takes it all away. I am praying you know that God *loves* you; He has *great* plans for you; and He's *cheering you on*.

The Lord GOD helps me; therefore I have not been disgraced; therefore I have set my face like a flint, and I know that I shall not be put to shame.

ISAIAH 50:7 ESV

God loves us as we are...not as we ought to be, because we are never going to be as we ought to be.

*Brennan Manning*

Shut off the distractions,

remove autopilot mode,

and *lean into Jesus.*

I am asking God to remind

you that He is always *near,*

always *listening,* and always

*pursuing* your heart.

Look carefully then how you walk,
not as unwise but as wise, making
the best use of the time, because
the days are evil.

EPHESIANS 5:15-16 ESV

Preach the gospel always,
and if necessary, use words.

*Francis of Assisi*

DaySpring

God is listening to your prayers! I am asking Him to *reveal* His plans to you, but sometimes silence is an invitation, not a dismissal. *Trust Him!*

Blessed are those who hunger
and thirst for righteousness,
for they shall be satisfied.

MATTHEW 5:6 ESV

Be much in secret prayer.
Converse less with man,
and more with God.

*George Whitefield*

I am praying God will
ease your anxieties
and bring rest to your
mind. His purpose for
your life is significant.

Many are the plans in a
person's heart, but it is the
LORD's purpose that prevails.

PROVERBS 19:21 NIV

The riddles of God are more satisfying
than the solutions of man.

G. K. Chesterton

I'm praying you'll experience God's *love,* *grace, and tenderness* in a fresh, new way today.

Having purified your souls by your obedience to the truth for a sincere brotherly love, love one another earnestly from a pure heart.

I PETER 1:22 ESV

Biblical love is not emotions or feelings, but attitudes and actions that seek the best interest of the other person.

*Jerry Bridges*

Your identity is not up
for negotiation! As you
sit with Jesus, I am praying
your wandering mind is put
at *ease* and that His Word
*sets you free.*

> You are a chosen people,
> a royal priesthood, a holy nation,
> God's special possession, that you
> may declare the praises of Him who
> called you out of darkness into
> His wonderful light.

I PETER 2:9 NIV

When the heart and the mind focus
on things unseen—that's when
there's a visible change in us.

*Ann Voskamp*

*Praying for you today—*
your Savior *loves* you and
desires to be near to you.
Reach out to Him; He is all
you need for *true peace.*

> God did this so that they would
> seek Him and perhaps reach out for
> Him and find Him, though He is not
> far from any one of us.
>
> ACTS 17:27 NIV

God surpasses our dreams when we
reach past our personal plans and
agenda to grab the hand of Christ
and walk the path He chose for us.
He is obligated to keep us
dissatisfied until we come to
Him and His plan for complete
satisfaction.

*Beth Moore*

I am praying God's Word will meet you *right where you are*. Life will sort itself out when you keep Jesus in the *center*.

The unfolding of your words gives light; it imparts understanding to the simple.

PSALM 119:130 NIV

Listen less to your own thoughts and more to God's thoughts.

*François Fénelon*

I am praying for you today. Let the *love* of Jesus lead the way and let His *kindness* guide you in all you say and do.

> This is my commandment, that you love one another as I have loved you. Greater love has no one than this, that someone lay down his life for his friends. You are my friends if you do what I command you.

JOHN 15:12-14 ESV

The first great and primary business to which I ought to attend every day is to have my soul happy in the Lord.

*George Mueller*

Pause and notice His *presence* in your life. I am praying for you as you go about your day; remember, *His timeline is perfect* and He never fails those *who seek Him.*

The LORD is good to those who wait for him, to the soul who seeks him.

LAMENTATIONS 3:25 ESV

The first act of love is always the giving of attention.

*Dallas Willard*

Your day is *brand-new,* your slate has been *wiped clean!* I am praying you remember the *grace* that has covered your past, present, and future. Let nothing hold you back from *confidently* running the race He has called you to!

Fear not, for you will not be put to shame; and do not feel humiliated, for you will not be disgraced; but you will forget the shame of your youth, and the reproach of your widowhood you will remember no more.

ISAIAH 54:4 NASB

Gaining a hopeful heart is not achieved by mere acquisition of knowledge; it is possible through the grace and love when leaning into the arms of our heavenly Father.

*Cleere Cherry*

I am praying you'll

never fear the mystery

of God, but rather let it

be an invitation for you to

*lean in and trust Him.*

Therefore do not worry about
tomorrow, for tomorrow will
worry about itself. Each day has
enough trouble of its own.

MATTHEW 6:34 NIV

Relying on God has to start all
over every day, as if nothing has
yet been done.

*C. S. Lewis*

I prayed today that fear would have no place in your life. Remember, your heavenly Father is *bigger* and *stronger* and *braver* than anything you may be facing today and in the future.

God has not given us a spirit of fear, but of power and of love and of a sound mind.

II TIMOTHY 1:7 NKJV

A man who is intimate with God will never be intimidated by men.

*Leonard Ravenhill*

DaySpring

I am praying that God will replace any feelings of worry or fear with His *peace and joy*. Reserve your energy for what matters and renew your mind in *Truth*.

We demolish arguments and every pretension that sets itself up against the knowledge of God, and we take captive every thought and make it obedient to Christ.

II CORINTHIANS 10:5 NIV

When obedience to God contradicts what I think will give me pleasure, let me ask myself if I love Him.

*Elisabeth Elliot*

I am praying that you take hold of the *free* and *beautiful* life God has promised you; *let all else break away.*

> For freedom Christ has set us free; stand firm therefore, and do not submit again to a yoke of slavery.
>
> GALATIANS 5:1 ESV

Punishment is never God's motivation. Freedom is.

*Lisa Bevere*

Your significance is not based on your schedule. I am praying God allows you to *rest* today (whether your calendar is packed or not).

> Teach us to number our days,
> that we may gain a heart of wisdom.
>
> PSALM 90:12 NIV

Seize the moment. Seize the
opportunities before you.
Don't put it off too long,
because you may not have as
much time as you think.

*Greg Laurie*

I am praying you are reminded of the secure *hope* you have in Jesus. He will iron out your doubts and replace your fear with *peace* if you let Him *guide the way*. Stay the course and *trust* His promises.

And now I want each of you to extend that same intensity toward a full-bodied hope, and keep at it till the finish. Don't drag your feet. Be like those who stay the course with committed faith and then get everything promised to them.

HEBREWS 6:11-12 THE MESSAGE

The world is changed by your example, not by your opinion.

*Bianca Olthoff*

The most *full* and *joyful* life is found in Jesus.

I am praying you take the time to sit with Him, be refreshed by His *strength* and renewed by His *grace*. Nothing else will satisfy your searching heart.

> You make known to me the path of life; in your presence there is fullness of joy; at your right hand are pleasures forevermore.
>
> PSALM 16:11 ESV

Our adversary majors in three things: noise, hurry, and crowds. If he can keep us engaged in "muchness" and "manyness," he will rest satisfied.

*Richard Foster*

*Anticipation* over anxiety—that is my prayer for you. I am asking God to flood your heart with *peace* and *trust*.

> Do not be anxious about anything, but in every situation, by prayer and petition, with thanksgiving, present your requests to God. And the peace of God, which transcends all understanding, will guard your hearts and your minds in Christ Jesus.
>
> PHILIPPIANS 4:6-7 NIV

Some people think God does not like to be troubled with our constant coming and asking. The way to trouble God is to not come at all.

*D. L. Moody*

I am praying God
silences your mind,
quiets your soul, and
unrushes your feet so
that you can experience
His presence. You will be
in awe of how He speaks.

Be still, and know that I am God.

PSALM 46:10 NIV

When God is silent, He is not still.

Tony Evans

I am praying
you'll *trust* the One
who formed you
to *protect* you.

Bear one another's burdens,
and so fulfill the law of Christ.

GALATIANS 6:2 ESV

When someone staggers, we help
steady the load. If he is straining,
we help bear the burden. And if he
stumbles, we lift him up.

*John MacArthur*

I'm asking God to
recalibrate your
thoughts and instead
fill your mind with
*comforting* thoughts of
His *love* and *peace*.

Be careful how you think; your
life is shaped by your thoughts.

PROVERBS 4:23 GNT

Gratefulness isn't hard.
Forgetting to be grateful
is what makes life hard.

*Ann Voskamp*

Jesus makes all things
*new*. I am praying God
will remind you of all
the potential you have,
and let you know that He's
*forgiven* all your mistakes.

Remember not the former things,
nor consider the things of old.
Behold, I am doing a new thing;
now it springs forth, do you not
perceive it? I will make a way in the
wilderness and rivers in the desert.

ISAIAH 43:18-19 ESV

Leave the broken, irreversible
past in God's hands, and step out
into the invincible future with Him.

*Oswald Chambers*

I am praying God *shines*
His light on you as you
*make His name known,*
giving Him all the *glory* and
*honor* as you run after Him.

It is the LORD your God you must
follow, and Him you must revere.
Keep His commands and obey Him;
serve Him and hold fast to Him.

DEUTERONOMY 13:4 NIV

Don't fall into the trap of studying
the Bible without doing what it says.

*Francis Chan*

I'm praying God will
allow you to take part in
His *miracles*. Keep going
where He is *leading* you.
He's got *big plans* for you,
and I can't wait to see them.

Truly, truly, I say to you,
whoever believes in me will
also do the works that I do; and
greater works than these will he do,
because I am going to the Father.

JOHN 14:12 ESV

Do your best while also remembering
your worth is not attached to what
you accomplish.

*Morgan Harper Nichols*

You can never be plucked or removed from your Savior's hands.

I am praying you are reminded of His *power, might, and strength*. There is nothing you will ever face that He does not have *victory* over. He is *above it all*.

One God and Father of all, who is over all and through all and in all.

EPHESIANS 4:6 NIV

The Bible says God never sleeps nor never slumbers...so there is no point in both of us staying awake.

*Christine Caine*

I am praying you never

lose hope or faith as you

walk through the hard times.

God is *at work* and He is

using all things for

*your good.*

Their work will be shown for what
it is, because the Day will bring it to
light. It will be revealed with fire,
and the fire will test the quality of
each person's work.

I CORINTHIANS 3:13 NIV

God shakes so that the things
that cannot be shaken will remain.

*Lisa Bevere*

I am praying God
helps you *trust Him*—
even when you don't
understand His methods.

Ah, Lord GOD! It is you who have made
the heavens and the earth by your
great power and by your outstretched
arm! Nothing is too hard for you.

JEREMIAH 32:17 ESV

It is possible for God to give you
favor with anyone at any time.
So if He is withholding it, trust Him.

*Jennie Allen*

God never leaves your side. I am praying He *leans in close* today, reminding you that He is *your home.* There is no greater *love* or *sacrifice* than His.

Behold, I have engraved you on the palms of my hands; your walls are continually before me.

ISAIAH 49:16 ESV

Our identity rests in God's relentless tenderness for us revealed in Jesus Christ.

*Brennan Manning*

If you sit with Him,
all else will find its
place. I am praying you
take the time to *draw near*
to Jesus, knowing that in
the solitude, *He paves the
way* for a successful life.

> Draw near to God, and he will
> draw near to you. Cleanse your
> hands, you sinners, and purify
> your hearts, you double-minded.

JAMES 4:8 ESV

Private worship excites
us for public worship.

*Matt Chandler*

Do not expect to know
all that lies ahead before
you take the next step.
His will is *pleasing,*
*perfect, and timely.*

> If we hope for what we do not see,
> we wait eagerly for it with
> patience and composure.
>
> ROMANS 8:25 AMP

His hands—they have us.
And haven't we learned?
His hands do not fail.

*Cleere Cherry*

God has a *wonderful*
life planned for you.
I am praying you'll *dream*
*big* and *walk courageously.*

"I know the plans I have for you,"
declares the LORD, "plans to prosper
you and not to harm you, plans to
give you hope and a future."

JEREMIAH 29:11 NIV

God's work done in God's way
will never lack God's supply.

*Hudson Taylor*

DaySpring

He is your *sun* and your *shield*. I am praying you run to Him when your mind wanders, *trust Him* when opposition comes, and *cling to Him* when hope feels far away. He will never disappoint you.

The LORD God is our sun and our shield. He gives us grace and glory. The LORD will withhold no good thing from those who do what is right.

PSALM 84:11 NLT

Friends, if we really and truly understood the mightiness and grace of the Father, our lives would look different in every way.

*Cleere Cherry*

I am praying God will take all your feelings of anger, hurt, pain, and frustration and fill you with a new spirit of *peace, hope, and joy.* I know it's hard to let this go, but God can *release you* from all of it.

> Good sense makes one slow to anger, and it is his glory to overlook an offense.
>
> PROVERBS 19:11 ESV

Stay focused instead of getting offended or off track by others.

*John Maxwell*

DaySpring

I am praying the
hardship, heartbreak,
and hopelessness you feel
in this moment is replaced
with *grace, gratitude, and
gumption* as you sit with the
King. He is *holding you close*
in this storm.

Why are you cast down, O my soul,
and why are you in turmoil within me?
Hope in God; for I shall again praise him,
my salvation and my God.

PSALM 43:5 ESV

The greater your knowledge of the goodness
and grace of God on your life, the more
likely you are to praise Him in the storm.

*Matt Chandler*

I am praying God will *reveal* Himself to you in a new way today, and that you will know, without a doubt, what *path* to take.

No one is more influential in your
life than you are. Because no one
talks to you more than you do.

*Paul Tripp*

Today, I prayed for

Jesus to take your

burdens, lift your fears,

and remind you that He is

*ultimately in control.*

Humble yourselves, therefore,
under the mighty hand of God so that
at the proper time he may exalt you,
casting all your anxieties on him,
because he cares for you.

I PETER 5:6-7 ESV

It's impossible to behold
what He has made and not be
humbled as the created.

*Ruth Chou Simons*

I am praying you *take* *hold* of every opportunity Jesus places before you, knowing that He will *guide you* every step of the way. Keep your eyes open and your feet ready. *He is at work.*

Then I heard the voice of the Lord, saying, "Whom shall I send, and who will go for us?" Then I said, "Here am I. Send me!"

ISAIAH 6:8 NIV

God's not asking for much. He's asking you to give up something you were never created to be so that you can become who He says you are.

*Todd White*

I'm asking God to give you the time to sit with Him today—and that you will be *refreshed* in His presence, knowing that He can make *anything possible.*

By the seventh day God had finished the work He had been doing; so on the seventh day He rested from all His work.

GENESIS 2:2 NIV

Unless and until we rest in God, we will never risk for God.

*Mark Buchanan*

You are *victorious* in Jesus. I am praying for you to remain *strong* and *confident* as you fight the good fight of *faith*, knowing that He is your *security*.

"No weapon that is formed against you will prosper; and every tongue that accuses you in judgment you will condemn. This is the heritage of the servants of the LORD, and their vindication is from Me," declares the LORD.

ISAIAH 54:17 NASB

Whatever fascinates you will guide you, so pray that the only thing that'll fascinate you is God and His marvelous glory.

*A. W. Tozer*

I am praying that your
heart *leans deeply*
into His, resting the
weight of your shoulders
at His feet and believing
that His *power is sufficient*
in your weakness.

Let us hold unswervingly to
the hope we profess, for He
who promised is faithful.

HEBREWS 10:23 NIV

There is not a single thing
that Jesus cannot change, control,
and conquer because He is the
living Lord.

*Franklin Graham*

I am praying you'll accept the *grace* He lavishes, and run hard after the *calling* He has placed on your life. *Peace* is yours when you *follow* Him.

> What you have learned and received and heard and seen in me—practice these things, and the God of peace will be with you.
>
> PHILIPPIANS 4:9 ESV

We cannot prioritize our doing before being, our assignment before healing, our service before freedom.

*Rebekah Lyons*

I am praying God will clearly show you the *divine placement* and *position* He has for you. Recognize His hand on your life and stand firmly in His *everlasting love*.

Therefore comfort each other and edify one another, just as you also are doing.

I THESSALONIANS 5:11 NKJV

My job is not to solve people's problems or make them happy, but to help them see the grace operating in their lives.

*Eugene H. Peterson*

You are *wildly,*
*unconditionally,*
and *eternally loved.*

Soak it up today!

See what great love the Father
has lavished on us, that we should
be called children of God! And that
is what we are! The reason the
world does not know us is that
it did not know Him.

I JOHN 3:1 NIV

I have given God countless
reasons not to love me.
None of them changed His mind.

*Paul Washer*

I am praying Jesus

will open up a window of

time for you to sit with

Him today. I asked Him to

give you *clarity, comfort,*

*and courage.*

> I am afraid that, as the serpent
> deceived Eve by his craftiness,
> your minds will be led astray
> from the simplicity and purity
> of devotion to Christ.
>
> II CORINTHIANS 11:3 NASB

Your perspective will either
become your prison or your passport.

*Steven Furtick*

You are not superhuman,
but the One that lives
inside of you is
*supernatural*. I am praying
you feel His *courage* and
*strength* within you;
you are not alone. *Trust*
*Him* to fight on your behalf!

So the sun stood still and the moon
stayed in place until the nation of
Israel had defeated its enemies.

JOSHUA 10:13 NLT

We were never called to do this in our
own strength. We need supernatural
empowerment from a supernatural God
to fulfill a supernatural calling.

*Christine Caine*

I am praying God will use you in *big* ways to reach people *everywhere* with His *love*. Let your kingdom perspective *guide the way*.

> The tongue has the power of life and death, and those who love it will eat its fruit.
>
> PROVERBS 18:21 NIV

Being made aware of the struggles of those around us allows us to speak life into them, not wallow in our own isolation, and be consistent in prayer and fellowship with one another.

*Cleere Cherry*

I am praying you

feel *secure* in your

*Rock* and *Redeemer*.

He is *restoring* your bones,

*revitalizing* your energy,

and *renewing* your hope.

These have come so that the
proven genuineness of your faith—
of greater worth than gold, which
perishes even though refined by fire—
may result in praise, glory and honor
when Jesus Christ is revealed.

I PETER 1:7 NIV

Instead of a river, God often gives us
a brook, which may be running today
and dried up tomorrow. Why? To teach
us not to rest in our blessings,
but in the blesser Himself.

*Arthur W. Pink*

I am praying God will
guide you as you make
plans. No matter what is
on your to-do list, remember
you can always *find rest,*
*hope,* and *peace* in Jesus.

But seek first the kingdom of
God and his righteousness, and all
these things will be added to you.

MATTHEW 6:33 ESV

The true God of your heart is
what your thoughts effortlessly
go to when there is nothing else
demanding your attention.

*Tim Keller*

I am praying you take great *comfort* in God— the One who made you and thinks you're an *amazing, one-of-a-kind, beautiful* person.

You formed my inward parts; you knitted me together in my mother's womb. I praise you, for I am fearfully and wonderfully made. Wonderful are your works; my soul knows it very well.

PSALM 139:13-14 ESV

We are made in the image of God; we carry within us the desire for our true life of intimacy and adventure. To say we want less than that is to lie.

*John Eldredge*

When you want to give up, lean in. I am praying for *strength* and *perseverance* for you. The race you are running is *purposeful* and *important;* He will help you with each step that you take.

Not that I have already obtained all this, or have already arrived at my goal, but I press on to take hold of that for which Christ Jesus took hold of me.

PHILIPPIANS 3:12 NIV

By perseverance the snail reached the ark.

*Charles Spurgeon*

*Gratitude* is the key to a *full life*. I am praying you are reminded of the *grace* He has *lavished* on you, the *truth* He has provided you, and the *love* He has extended to you.

Rooted and built up in him
and established in the faith,
just as you were taught,
abounding in thanksgiving.

COLOSSIANS 2:7 ESV

Jesus is moved to happiness every
time He sees that you appreciate
what He has done for you.

*Ole Hallesby*

You were made to *shine!* I am praying God's *light* will *fill you* until you *overflow*.

In the same way, let your light shine before others, that they may see your good deeds and glorify your Father in heaven.

MATTHEW 5:16 ESV

Hide yourself in God, so when a man wants to find you he will have to go there first.

*Shannon L. Alder*

I prayed God would

*renew* your spirit

today.  You are God's

*masterpiece, fearfully*

and *wonderfully* made.

> Put on the new self, created
> after the likeness of God in true
> righteousness and holiness.
>
> EPHESIANS 4:24 ESV

Believe me, you cannot stand
still in your souls. Habits of
good or evil are daily strengthening
in your hearts. Every day you are
either getting nearer to God,
or further off.

*J. C. Ryle*

I am praying God will
*fill your heart* with His
*presence* today, replacing
any dull spots with His
*bright, shining light.*

This is what the Sovereign LORD
says: Look! I am going to put breath
into you and make you live again!

EZEKIEL 37:5 NLT

But if you find yourself
experiencing a desire to seek God,
we have great news for you: God is
already at work in you.

*Henry Blackaby*

I am praying God *reveals* Himself to you during the *stillness* of your morning, the *quietness* of your midday walk, and the *calmness* of your commute home.

Being still and opening up our heart to Jesus does not just keep us from becoming crazy people; it reveals to our heart those in our path that need to be loved.

*Cleere Cheery*

When you sit still with

the Giver, you remember

that everything is a *gift*.

I am asking God to *quiet* your

heart and *reassure* you that

He will provide everything

you need in order to do what

He is asking you to do.

God is able to bless you abundantly,
so that in all things at all times,
having all that you need, you will
abound in every good work.

II CORINTHIANS 9:8 NIV

If we have the audacity to ask,
God has the ability to perform.

*Steven Furtick*

Today I'm praying God will remind you who He says you are. He says you're *loved, extraordinary, seen, chosen, victorious,* and so much more! So don't believe anything else you hear.

> For we are God's handiwork, created in Christ Jesus to do good works, which God prepared in advance for us to do.
>
> EPHESIANS 2:10 NIV

God doesn't always make His will clear because He values our being transformed more than our being informed.

*Jon Boom*

DaySpring

I am praying you'll

be *comforted* by God's

promises to give you

*strength, comfort, love,*

*grace,* and so much more.

And He never breaks

His promises.

Let the word of Christ dwell in you
richly in all wisdom, teaching and
admonishing one another in psalms and
hymns and spiritual songs, singing
with grace in your hearts to the Lord.

COLOSSIANS 3:16 NKJV

Christ is a substitute for
everything, but nothing is
a substitute for Christ.

*Harry Ironside*

I'm praying God will *reveal Himself* to you in *new, exciting* ways today.

> Hold on to instruction,
> do not let it go; guard it well,
> for it is your life.
>
> PROVERBS 4:13 NIV

Our spiritual maturity will never exceed our knowledge of the Bible.

*Albert Mohler*

I am praying God will

erase all the crazy standards

and labels placed on you and

help you stay focused on what

He asks—that you may do

*justly, love mercy,* and *walk*

*humbly* with your God.

That is a recipe for a *healthy,*

*fruitful life.*

He has shown you, O man, what is good; and what
does the LORD require of you but to do justly, to
love mercy, and to walk humbly with your God?

MICAH 6:8 NKJV

Ten minutes spent in the presence
of Christ every day, aye, two minutes,
will make the whole day different.

*Henry Drummond*

How *marvelous* that you need not travel to *experience* God's presence—He is alive in you! I am praying you feel *strengthened* today as you tap into His *power, love,* and the *peace* of a sound mind.

Blessed is the one who trusts in the LORD, whose confidence is in Him.

JEREMIAH 17:7 NIV

We need no wings to go in search of Him, but have only to look upon Him present within us.

*Teresa of Ávila*

Do you see His hand at work? Do you *trust* what He is doing? Praying that your *peace of mind* is secured in Him, painting the world around you with *color* and seeing the possibility and opportunity that is present in all circumstances.

The LORD will give strength to His people;
the LORD will bless His people with peace.

PSALM 29:11 NKJV

A mind at peace beautifies the
plainest surroundings and even
in the hardest conditions.

*J. R. Miller*

*Jesus is your guide.*
He leads you to spacious
places. His way is sure.
I am praying for you'll be
*strengthened* by His presence
as your loving Shepherd.

> The LORD is my shepherd,
> I lack nothing. He makes me
> lie down in green pastures,
> He leads me beside quiet waters.
>
> PSALM 23:1-2 NIV

There are no experts in the company
of Jesus. We are all beginners,
necessarily followers, because we
don't know where we are going.

*Eugene Peterson*

Problems will always
exist but *peace* is
always within reach!
How gracious is God to be
our *refuge* and our Savior.
Praying you are reminded
that He is in *control!*

The LORD is good, a stronghold
in the day of trouble; and He
knows those who trust in Him.

NAHUM 1:7 NKJV

Peace is within reach, not for
lack of problems, but because
of the presence of a sovereign Lord.

*Max Lucado*

I am praying you find *peace* in your present by remembering where you are headed—you are a citizen of heaven. Remember who you are and find *peace* until you get where you *belong*.

> Above all, you must live as citizens of heaven, conducting yourselves in a manner worthy of the Good News about Christ.
>
> PHILIPPIANS 1:27 NLT

Inner peace doesn't come from getting what we want, but from remembering who we are.

*Marianne Williamson*

When life throws us curveballs, remember there is never panic in heaven. I am praying for you as you take your bricks out of your book bag and give them to your *heavenly Father* to carry. Travel lightly through today.

Anxiety weighs down the heart,
but a kind word cheers it up.

PROVERBS 12:25 NIV

God has no problems, only plans.
There is never panic in heaven.

*Corrie ten Boom*

I am praying for you as you go about your day, following the path He has for you, and taking on new *challenges* and *opportunities!* Eyes up, good things ahead.

Follow the life-map absolutely,
keep an eye out for the signposts,
His course for life set out in the
revelation to Moses; then you'll
get on well in whatever you do
and wherever you go.

I KINGS 2:3 THE MESSAGE

How happy we are when we realize
that He is responsible, that He goes
before, that goodness and mercy
shall follow us.

*Lettie Cowman*

God's eyes are on your
life—your past, your
present, and your future.
I am praying His *strong*
hand is your *guide*.

So if you're serious about living
this new resurrection life with
Christ, act like it. Pursue the
things over which Christ presides.
Don't shuffle along, eyes to the
ground, absorbed with the things
right in front of you.

COLOSSIANS 3:1 THE MESSAGE

He that loves works out good to
those that He loves, as He is able.
God's power and will are equal;
what He wills He works.

*John Owen*

Just as the sun continues to rise every morning, God is worth *trusting* every day. I am praying God will give you the *courage* to step out and the *perseverance* to walk forth, remembering your *faithful* Father will never disappoint you.

Let us hold fast the confession of our hope without wavering, for he who promised is faithful.

HEBREWS 10:23 ESV

Don't be afraid to step out and trust God. He is more faithful than the rising of the sun.

*Kari Jobe*

Jesus is *faithful* to complete His work in you. I am praying you are not discouraged by the hiccups of the here and now but are reminded of the *life* He has prepared for you in *eternity*.

> So flee youthful passions and pursue righteousness, faith, love, and peace, along with those who call on the Lord from a pure heart.
>
> II TIMOTHY 2:22 ESV

Peace convicts, forgives, and delivers you.
Peace will finish his work in you.
Peace will welcome you into glory,
where Peace will live with you in
peace and righteousness forever.

*Paul David Tripp*

I'm praying God helps
you navigate your
difficult relationships,
giving you the words and
actions to share *His love*
and *heal hearts.*

Let your gentleness be evident
to all. The Lord is near.

PHILIPPIANS 4:5 NIV

It is only imperfection that
complains of what is imperfect.
The more perfect we are, the more
gentle and quiet we become toward
the defects of others.

*François Fénelon*